THE OUTCOME OF OUR CHOICES

Written By

GERALDINE MCNAIR

outskirts
press

Dedicated to all female teens and Ladies

Table of Contents

Dear Friend,

Have you ever made decisions and regretted it later? How many times have you made choices centered around emotions, impulse, anxiety, stress, or peer pressure? When you reflect on your past, has any of the decisions you made cost you heartache and pain, financial debt, stress, emptiness, loneliness, feelings of failure, low self-esteem, embarrassment etc.

I am not saying all choices we have made are bad; some choices in life were good and edifying to us. However, we must be true to ourselves and admit that we have made some poor choices in life that brought about some consequences we did not bargain for.

I believe every woman on the planet has experienced making bad choices in life especially when it comes to sexual morality! Yes, you know that thing that is popular, that very thing which for most of us has changed our complete world!

It has affected our thought process; it has caused us to compromise and for some it has changed even who we are and who God purposed us to be.

I never knew the power of sexual immorality until later in life. This thing is deadly, powerful and has even influenced people to have a sex change. It has power to cause men to be lovers of men and women to be lovers of women. The act of this immorality has broken and damaged many marriages and families. Unless we the people of God get delivered from it, there is no way we can make a better impact in the world in which we live.

I pray that by the time you are done reading my book, your attitude toward sexual morality will be different. No more will you be enslaved by immoral action. No more will the thoughts and ways of man affect your decision to hold onto your morals and cherish your values or standards.

Who Are You?

1 Peter 2:9
But you are a chosen people, a royal priesthood, a holy nation, God's special possession, that you may declare the praises of him who called you out of darkness into his wonderful light.

Many of us do not know who we are. Ladies, I cannot make you see how important and valuable you are. You must stand on **1 Peter 2:9** and know your worth. I will explain more about this scripture later as you continue to read. In addition to the scripture, God made each of us unique in Him. He designed us to be beautiful, smart, intellectual, creative, and skillful; He created us with a womb, and gave us a nurturing spirit.

Why do you think He created Eve for Adam? It was because God saw that Adam needed a companion, someone to walk by his side to be there through the rough times as well as the good times. God knew that Eve would be a nurturer, a woman filled with compassion and strong willed. When a woman has her mind made up, it is hard to convince her to do otherwise. In the bible, Eve was able to convince Adam to do the wrong thing, and later they both paid a costly price for their sin. They were thrown out of the garden and never to return.

My point in saying this, is that we as women are stronger than our men. They may be stronger physically, but women have had the power over men for decades. We can seduce them, trap them, we can deceive them, build their self-esteem and break them down all at the same time. We can intoxicate them with our red dress, the stiletto shoes, the walk, the seductive words, our hair and our intellect is enough to rock any man's world.

However, ladies this is not what God created us for! We are to walk better than the ways of the world. We are a royal priesthood, a holy nation, a peculiar people meaning that God himself holds us in high esteem. He sees us as somebody of great value to show forth the excellence of Him!

Do not let the choices you make in life define who you are unless the decisions you made are positive. The reason why it is so important we know who we are is because, once you learn your worth in Christ, and who owns you, then your choices become **limited**. Did I just use the word **limited**? Yes ma'am! Here me ladies with limitations also comes **restraints!!!**

When we allow ourselves to be governed and restrained by God, it means that we do not belong to ourselves. Therefore, decisions or choices we make should include Him and be restrained by Him whenever necessary. Think back on the many times in life you made important choices or decisions without God. Did you later suffer for the choices you made? If you could go back into your past, would you have made a different decision? Are you still living out the consequences of poor choices you made in your past?

One topic I really want to deal with is Sex over marriage, which will be discussed later. However, upon my completion of the topic "Who

Are You?", I just want to encourage you to learn about your self-worth from our Spiritual Father. Let us stop beating ourselves up with poor decisions that we make. It is time for every pre-teen, teenage - girl and woman to make better choices for your life so that you can begin to experience what God truly has for you.

If someone ask you right now **Who are You?** What would your answer be besides giving them your first and last name or telling them where you work or your favorite color, or what school you attend. Those answers would only tell us a little about you. However, where is the character description? Do you know why God created you? What is your purpose here on earth? Now with all of this in mind, ask yourself again, who am I? If you are still having problems with this question, memorize 1 Peter 2:9 and then take it to the next level and ask God what is your purpose here on earth, and how can you be of better service to him?

Which Should Come First, Marriage or Sex???

Genesis 2:24

Therefore, a man shall leave his father and mother and be joined to his wife and they shall become one flesh

Marriage should come before sex, but it seems that most people have chosen sex before marriage. I have observed unmarried couples for years and I noticed that most of these couples tend to stay together for years until they say those two magic words **"I DO"**.

It amazes me how they lived together for five-ten years, but divorce after being married. I used to often wonder why people refused to get married first before living together. There are all kinds of reasons people choose to live together first: lack of finances, sex, insecurity, loneliness, no strings attached, testing the waters of marriage, making pre-mature decisions together, like purchasing a home or vehicle or having a baby. I am sure there are other reasons I have not listed.

On average, researchers concluded that, couples who lived together before they tied the knot saw a 33 percent higher rate of divorce

than those who waited to live together after they were married. Part of the problem was that cohabiters studies suggested, "slid into" marriage without much consideration.

What really saddens my heart is that some of us as Christians have joined the ways of the world when it comes to the sacredness of marriage. We have forgotten about God and focusing on gratifying the flesh. We have become oblivious to the word of God, and value the ways and thoughts of society.

God is a God of order and in His word, He specifically stated

Let everything be done in decency and in order.
1Corinthians 14:40

He also says in Isaiah 55:8 My thoughts are not your thoughts, neither are your ways my ways declare the Lord.

Listen up ladies, it is not the will of God that we should shack up with any man.

If he is truly the man that God has chosen for you, then he will wait for you. If he cannot wait for you, then it proves two things about him. He is not your man, and he does not have any respect for you or the word of God inside of you.

Genesis 2:24 clearly states that a man shall leave his father and mother and be joined to his wife and they shall become one flesh.

This scripture did not say his girlfriend, or significant other but his wife.

To the pre-teens and teens reading this book. I know most of you are not considering living with a male because you are not old enough to live on your own. However, a lot of you are having sex. Whether you did it once or you do it often, does not matter. What does matter is that you are setting yourself up to be hurt. Without knowing it, you are stripping yourself of your worth and who God called you to be. If you do not remember anything else from this page you are reading, please remember this, those boys do not see your value. They are not looking at you as the queen they would like to marry later in life. Trust me if they sleep with you, they have slept with others before you, so what makes you think that they see you differently?

Some of you may not know that sex among teen boys is nothing but a game! Boys are still making bets with each other to see if they can convince you to have sex with them. They often- times compete, to see which guy will score first with the girl they are dating. Most males are not emotional when it comes to sexual intercourse the way females are. When a teen girl or woman is sexually involved with a man, her heart is wrapped into the guy. She fully commits herself to him and gives her heart totally to the relationship. Females are more prone to suffer heart breaks when separation takes place. We are so passionate and affection- ate that even if we are not sexually involved, our heart still can become broken once the relationship has dissolved.

I will not say all, but most males can shake off a broken relation- ship, a lot quicker than we as females. They can sleep with you and date you for several years and act like they do not know you anymore, and date someone else. Have you ever experienced that? I have seen several people, both girls and women who were devasted by males who either stole their virginity or deceived the female into believing that he really cared about her and wanted only her. After getting what he wanted or after getting bored with her, he then turns to someone else he thinks is more exciting. Not all, but most males tend to run after they find out that his significant other is now pregnant with his baby.

Open your eyes, do not take this offensively, but take it as words of wisdom. You are better than this, and its nothing wrong with **saying no! not until I 'am married!!!** Condoms, birth control, IUD's and other contraceptives used to practice safe sex is not 100% guaranteed, but abstinence (**not having sex at all**) is the safest way. Abstinence from sex prevents you from sexual diseases and it also helps you to walk away from bad relationships. I am saying this, because when you do not have a soul tie with them, which involves sex, there is a better chance you tend to be stronger emotionally if you need to cut the relationship. Above all, abstinence shows that you respect your body as the temple of God and your self-worth. If you are a Christian, it shows that you believe in the standards of God and not society.

When we are sexually active it is hard for us to make sound decisions. Being emotionally tied up in a relationship, hinders you from making the right choice. My mom used to tell me, **"don't get caught up with these men because you won't be able to see the trees from the forest"**. I never really understood what she meant by that statement until later in life. I have never had sex with a man, but I have come close a couple of times. I was emotionally tied to a couple of men that I almost slipped with. There were times I compromised just to please them. Deep down within, I knew one person that was not good for me to be with, because he always had sex on his mind. No matter how many times I said I wanted to wait until marriage, he would try to get me to compromise through sexual foreplay! Oops did I just say the word foreplay!!! Do not judge me, stop acting as though you never experienced it. Maybe you have not if you are eleven or twelve and if so, that is great! However, I need to speak on this one, because this is where it all begins, and this is how most women and teens end up pregnant!

What is sexual foreplay- It is sexual activity that takes place before having intercourse, such as fondling or caressing your partner. This is an extremely dangerous zone to tamper with because it is a sure way **that can** and **will lead** you to having sex with your partner. Some people say foreplay is wrong, while others say it is okay if there is no penetration involved.

However, we cannot follow what society says, because if we leave it up to them, they will take us straight to hell! We must use wisdom and follow what the bible says about sexual activity. Many of us may try to justify sexual foreplay, but in God's eyesight it is wrong, and God is not pleased with Christians being participants of this!

1 Corinthians 6:18 says **Flee from sexual immorality**. Every other sin a person commits is outside the body, but the **sexually immoral person** sins against his own body.

Galatians 5:19-21 Now the works of the flesh are evident: **sexual immorality, impurity,** sensuality, idolatry, sorcery, enmity, strife, jealousy, fits of anger, rivalries, dissensions, divisions, envy, drunkenness, **orgies**, and things like these. I warn you as I warned you before, that those who do such things will not inherit the kingdom of God.

We must get connected to what the bible says about sexual immorality. We cannot get caught up into the advice of the world. Remember ladies, we do not have to answer to man for our wrong doings, but we do have to answer to God!!! Your momma may not catch you; your children may not see what you do behind closed doors, but God sees everything, and He is the one we need to be concerned about.

Let us get back to the friend I was telling you about earlier, you know the one that tried to convince me to have intercourse with him. He tried everything, he even bought himself a used Lexus and gave it to me to drive every day to work, while he used my old Toyota Corolla that was on its last leg. When my co-workers saw me pulling into the parking lot they begin admiring and congratulating me on my new car. I quickly corrected them and let them know it was not mine. I told them it belonged to my boyfriend, who let me borrow his car, until

I got my car repaired. They all started looking at me in a strange way and at one another. Finally, someone blurted out that I must be giving him some, since I had his car! It was this comment that really made me mad, but it also got me thinking. I started realizing that these are the ways of the world. Men buy you things, give you lavishing gifts, give you money to get your hair done, and in return you are supposed to have sex with them as a thank you. When I realized that my friend, the man I thought I would marry someday, was guilty of all these things I just mentioned, I realized that he was not the one. On top of this I caught him cheating on me with someone else because I refuse to have sex with him.

This is what my mom was trying to warn me about. See when a man wine and dine you, buy you gifts, let you drive his car around, buy you clothes you did not ask for, watch out!!! Ask yourself what is the motive? Is it because he really loves you and wants to give you his best? Is it because he wants you to feel like you belong to him? Is it because he feels he deserves to have you even if it means you compromising your morals? I realized that this relationship for me was toxic because it was going against my standards, morals, and my self-worth. I have always been taught by my mother to wait until I am married and do not make the same mistakes she made. I am so glad I listened to her because it has certainly made my life simple.

When I get married, I will not have bags I am bringing into the relationship from another man who scarred me. I will not find myself comparing my husband to another man I slept with. My Godmother who lives in Charlotte taught me that when you sleep with a man, you develop a soul tie with him. Once a man penetrates us, we become emotionally tied to him. when a woman is verbally or physically abused by a man, it is hard for her to leave him when there are soul ties involved. You also find yourself making decisions that you would not ordinarily make. This guy that I was so madly in love with also tried to get me to buy a house with him. He told me, he would let me move in the house first, and then he would move in later after we got married. He knew the right words to use with me. He knew I was not comfortable with the idea of us living together before marriage. Therefore he tried to deceive me, but it did not work!!!

I thank God for wise counsel because a marriage counselor told me that you never buy a home or vehicle with someone you have not married. Once you sign the dotted lines, you are trapped, and you will be just as responsible for the thing you purchased with him. My counselor made me realize that if we broke up later, that this could end up in a disaster for me financially and it could mess up my credit as well.

Where am I going with all this? Why am I revealing myself? It is because I do care for young girls and women across the nation. I wish every female could read my book; it is time out for us as ladies to continue compromising our self-worth. It is time out for teenagers giving away their virginity just because they are curious and want to know what it feels like. God did not design sexual intercourse or sexual foreplay for teens and singles to enjoy. Sex was designed to be sacred between married couples only. God purposely made it this way so they would be fruitful and multiply and blessed the earth with more children.

To all teenagers, I know you have heard these lines before: well if we love each other, what is wrong with us expressing our love for one another. You may have heard someone say that it is nothing wrong with two people having sex because that is what people do when they are in love.

To my single adult ladies, I am sure you have heard someone say the only way you can keep a man, is to have sex with him because men have sexual needs. If you do not satisfy his physical needs, then he will eventually leave you.

Sad to say most of it, but not all of it is true! Men do have sexual desires and needs and most of them will not stay true and committed to a relationship without sex involved. However, there are a few men that still exist that want the same thing a woman with morals and values want. They too would like to have intercourse with the woman they decide to marry. Some men find it an honor and privilege to be with a woman of high standards, because they do not run across women that

are still trying to stay **celibate** (virgin or abstaining from sex). I believe that we could have more men with respect for women, if we would not make it so easy for them. They do not respect the principle that sex was created by God for married people, because we do not reverence it. Men do not respect us and see our value and worth because we do not see it. They do not see us as pearls or ladies that respect our bodies because we do not. **We cannot expect them to see what we do not see!!!**

Come on ladies and teens, come out of the forest so you can see the trees as my mom would put it! Open your eyes and look around you. Look at your big sister, aunt, your mother, church friends, school friends, co-workers, close friends that you have been knowing forever! How many of them have children without a husband?

I am not trying to be condescending but let us look at this picture together. Can I get blatantly real with you sisters? Think about it, you have had sex multiple times, and some of you have had children. I decided to not have sex and totally cut out sexual foreplay or any type of sexual activity that may lead to sex out of my life completely. I have made celibacy a practice that I intend to keep until I am married. I have never been married, and some of you have never gotten married either. You may have shacked with someone for several years and maybe you are still living that lifestyle. However, although you may call him your husband, in God's eyesight he is not. He is just someone that you have a sexual soul tie with. The only way he will become your husband is if you are willing to do it the right way and that is to marry him!!!

What is my point, where am I going with this? My point is this – Sex or no sex we both do not have a husband. We are still singled and if your significant other were to die right now, you are not entitled to any of his belongings because legally you are not his wife. What is my point? My point is why not do it the right way instead of doing it our way and having to pay the consequences later. In my opinion living with a man just to feel like we got a man or to feel like we are in a marriage is not the real thing. Calling myself married based on a living together situation that is not sanctified or approved by God is not something I want for me. Therefore, I am good with the waiting, because I know he only has his best for me, and it will be worth the wait!

To the ladies and teens, who have suffered humiliation, wrongful judgement due to walking in celibacy hold your head up! I used to be ashamed of my virginity after graduating from high school. I did not want anyone to know, because I was afraid of people accusing me of being a lesbian. I did not want them to criticize me or think different about me, so I was careful to not mention it to anyone.

It is hurtful when people do not respect your standards and accuse you of being something you are not. Believe me, I am talking from experience, but now I do not care anymore. All I care about is pleasing God with my life. When you get to that level spiritually, sex or sexual foreplay must go in Jesus name! We can no longer be participants of those things that grieve God!

To My Teens!!!

Where is that teenage boy, that told you that if two people really love each other they should express it by having sex! You are sixteen or seventeen and have not finished high school yet. You are stuck with his baby and the boy that got you pregnant is now dating one of your friends as if nothing ever happened between the two of you! Who is this boy, you gave your virginity to, and he gave you a Sexual disease in return! Who is this boy that never took the time to learn the real you and get to know your worth! This young boy that does not know you, distracted you and got your goods. You gave him your body for free, and he did not have to pay for it by way of respect.

1 Corinthians 6:18-19
sexual immorality is a sin against your own body. Don't you realize that your body is the temple of the Holy Spirit, who lives in you and was given to you by God, you do not belong to yourself."

To the Ladies of our Nation!

Where is that grown man, who wined you and dined you, bought you a car, clothes, shoes, helped you with your rental payments, gave you money for a fresh hair due. You had his baby later and your child is now six years old and has not seen her father since she was two. Where is he? Where is the man who tickled your ears with fancy words? You remember how he told you, "you are the only one for me baby; it is just me and you." Yes, the man who told you, he would be there for you; the man you have soul ties with is now married to someone else, but you have his baby!!! You fight with him for child support, because now he is married to someone else and has kids with her. Some men are inconsiderate and oblivious to the fact that they do have a child by you. They will quit their jobs and work a job that will give them cash, just to keep the government from tracing their income; this way they will not have to give you a dime of their money!

Matthew 7:6 says **"Do not give what is holy to the dogs; nor cast your pearls before swine, lest they trample them under their feet, and turn and tear you in pieces.**

You do not deserve this teens and ladies for you are more than conquerors through Christ Jesus who love you! I have seen too many young teens ruin their lives with teen pregnancy; I have seen too many sisters in Christ left to raise their kids alone with their hearts broken over a man they thought was the one!

Priscilla Shirer, a minister of the gospel said these very words: "Sin will take you further then you ever intended to go. It will keep you longer than you intended to stay, and it will cost you way more than you ever intended to pay!!! Wow this statement by her is so true about sin. I do not know about you, but I can definitely relate to her on this one.

I am Afraid of Being Alone

Isaiah 41:10
So do not fear, for I am with you; do not be dismayed, for I am your God. I will strengthen you and help you; I will uphold you with my righteous right hand.

Being afraid of being alone invites insecurity, compromising standards, depression and fear which are not of God. Have I ever been lonely or felt lonely? Yes of course I have. There were times in my life I wanted to celebrate the 4th of July or New Year's with my significant other and not with my Godchildren or sisters in Christ! There were times I wished I were with Mr. Right at the movies instead of with my best friend or play sister or Godchild. However, the one thing I did not and do not entertain is depression.

I have never been married and I have never had any children. Having children is not hard to do because if I really wanted to, I could have compromised in my past relationships and gotten pregnant once or twice. However, I am proud to say I practice celibacy and I made a vow to God that I would not have sex with a man before I am married. Wait a minute, do not judge me. I am not a Lesbian; trust me I have come close to having sex a few times with a couple of men I dated from the past. Did I want to experience it? Yes, I wanted to experience it, but my inner man knew that it was the wrong thing to do. I often told myself that if I let my guards down, I would regret it for the rest of my life. I believe that was the Holy Spirit speaking to me. He would often remind me that I was playing with fire whenever I found myself compromising in the least bit.

Draw the Line!!!

I remember the very last time I came close to having sex, I decided then I needed to draw the line. Most men do not draw lines. If you are willing to sleep with them, they are not going to resist you. We are all different as women, and there comes a time you must do what is best for you, and the person you are dating. I never thought I would share this, but I even made a vow to God that I would not French kiss (tongue kiss) another man until I am married. I know this sounds crazy and over the top! However, like I said you must do what is best for you! It was French kissing that oftentimes drove me and my partner into sexual activity (foreplay). All it takes is a passionate kiss behind closed doors where no one can see you and then one thing leads to another. If you are not strong enough, you will find yourself having sex. I was told by a male friend of mine, once you start having sex, you will not be able to quit so easily. I was told that sex is like eating potato chips; you cannot eat just one chip without going back for more!!! Therefore, my solution to all of this is that we **DRAW THE LINE!!!** If you are not practicing celibacy, start now; it is never too late to please God!!! Even some of the strongest people have given into fornication. Prophets, Pastors, Evangelist, Sunday school teachers, ministers, church people have fallen in this area. Sex has no respect of person and if you entertain it, you will become trapped like so many others.

Yes, giving up French kissing was a big decision for me, and I knew it was going to cost me. This decision meant I was decreasing my chance of having a steady relationship. It also meant that some men would judge me and assume that I must be a lesbian since I do not participate in sexual activity or passionate kissing. Regardless, as I look back on the lives of other females in Christ, many of them have crossed the line. They were sexually active with the men they had a steady relationship with, but what did it prove. Because as I recall, most of them did not marry the guy they slept with. I know someone, who was in an adulterous relationship for several long years, but now they are no longer seeing each other. What is my point? What am I saying? **ITS NOT WORTH IT!!!** In the end you will still be alone if he is **Not Mr. Right!** Most of the times the men we sleep with are only place holders for the **real man!!!**

Oh, and about those place holders, watch out because the real man can not take his place until you have gotten rid of your place holders. Teens! This is **not for you,** this is for the single adults who want to settle down with one person and commit themselves in marriage.

I learned from my Spiritual mother that a man cannot control you if you do not sleep with him. If you sleep with a man, he will try to control you and you will always find yourself trying to please him. When you are sexually involved with a man, you suddenly, become passive towards his actions. If Friday evenings are his normal time to be with you and he gives you an excuse for not coming, you may accept it without questioning him. However, if you are not sleeping with him, you are going to question him and maybe do a little investigating. All men know that if you sleep with him that helps to give him control of you. Most of them began to think they own you.

As singles we can overcome loneliness! It is true that an idle mind is a devil workshop. If we do not occupy our minds with constructive works, and activities to do, then we can find ourselves in places we do not need to be in and doing things we should not be doing.

There is so much we can focus on doing to better ourselves and our community. There is so much work needed in the Kingdom!!! We get bored and lonely because we do not apply ourselves constructively. We get lonely because we do not spend enough time meditating on the word of God and bringing others to Christ. If we are about our Father's business, there will be little time for loneliness. Yes, I know as a woman you do at times long for companionship from a man. Trust me I am not oblivious to this, and I can very well relate to my statement about companionship. All I am saying is, what do we do now? Do we just mope around in depression or should we try to enjoy our lives as singles until we do meet Mr. Right. As single females, we can concentrate on getting our finances in order, paying on those credit cards we ran up, changing bad habits and replacing them with better ones. We can work on our attitudes, personality, and temperament so that when we meet our King, we will not drive the man insane with our insecurities and disorderly lifestyle.

To the Teens!

Teens! Listen up stay focus on your school, get involve in a sport or one of the clubs at your school. Find something constructive to do with your time when you have no homework. Make time for God; read your bible and pray diligently to God. Ask him to give you the strength to not be like those other fast girls in your school. Take it from me, you will still have plenty time for sex later but that should not be your focus at age 15 or 17 or 18 or 21!!! Sex was not made for teens to enjoy but for the married people only. Be careful to not bite off more than you can chew teenagers. Remember there are consequences for sins we commit, especially when we know better.

James 1:15 says Then desire when it has conceived gives birth to sin, and sin when it is fully grown brings forth death.

To the Ladies!

Please keep yourselves busy focusing on making you a better you by doing positive things in life. As a single woman, I still have wants; I have desires and emotions. I am not a robot; I am not perfect, and I do not have all the right answers. However, I can say that between working as a teacher for the child development arena, running my Heart of Worship dance school, pastoring over the children's ministry for my church, writing sermons, books and teaching dance classes has been enough to keep me busy from having an idle mind. The other important thing we must do and should place it as top priority is give God some of our time in reading the bible and studying his word. As you can see, there is little time for depression or loneliness in my life. When I feel like it, I find the time to do something fun that I enjoy doing alone or with others. Sometimes, I enjoy doing things alone because I need that time just for me. If you are looking for a man to complete you, or make you happy, then you are not ready for marriage. You must get to a point in your life, where you become complete in Christ and with or without a man you are happy within yourself.

Attacks on the Dreams

I believe that all females who are interested in the opposite sex are attacked in our dreams with lustful thoughts. We may dream about having sex with the boy we have a heavy crush on or with the man of our dreams. Did you know that when you entertain thoughts of sexual activity that you are in sin? Some people think that if you do not commit the act in the physical it is okay, and you have not sinned. This belief is incorrect; if you are thinking of hurting someone and you never did it in the physical it is still wrong. It was a sinful thought that was in your heart so therefore, you need to repent and ask God to forgive you. If you do not repent and ask God to forgive you, then you are at risk of committing an act that you may not be ready to pay the penalty for. This also applies to sexual thoughts in our minds. We can undress a person, commit sexual foreplay, and have sex with them in our thoughts. We can have dreams upon dreams about physical intimacy with someone we are not married to and it is all wrong. God is not pleased with this. The bible says in **Matthew 15:18-19 But the things that proceed out of the mouth come from the heart, and those defile the man. For out of the heart come evil thoughts, murders, adulteries, fornications (sexual activity), thefts, false witness, slanders.**

When we sin on the outside, we are showing others that this is something that was already in our hearts to do. We have already sinned on the inside and now it is coming out of us! We must be careful with what we watch on TV and what we listen to in terms of our music selection. What is in the heart comes out of the mouth and in our action. We must realize that we do become connected to what we feed our spirit in the physical and in the spiritual. God has asked us to resist the temptation by running away from it. We are not supposed to see how close we can get to it, before we get burnt by it, or fall into the trap of it. Fleeing starts with avoiding the thoughts about the wrong action.

Proverbs 23:7 says So as a man thinketh in his heart so is he.

I do not know about you, but I want to be free in my mind of lustful thoughts or any thoughts that are not pleasing unto God. When it is time for me to go to bed, I must speak out loud over my mind. There is power in our words for the believers. If you are not born again in Christ this may not work for you. However, pray to God and speak that your mind is covered with the blood of Jesus. Tell the devil he has no authority over your mind and that your soul belongs to God. Speak out loud that your dreams will be filled with the peace and thoughts of God and there is no room for lust of any kind. Play your bible app from your phone; listen to the word of God. You can also play worship music and let it minister to you while sleeping. If you do this constantly, you will find that your thoughts and dreams will be pure.

When you wake up the next morning, you will hear certain Christian songs still playing in your head or your Spirit man will be filled with the word of God. A good book of the bible to listen to while sleeping is Proverbs because this book is like an instructional manual that tells us how to live our lives. It is great for gaining wisdom and knowledge of the word. There is no sugar coating in Proverbs. I love this book of the bible because it makes you face reality, brings conviction and it causes you to evaluate yourself and where your heart is.

Wait on God for Best Results!

Isaiah 40:31

But they who wait for the Lord shall renew their strength; they shall mount up with wings like eagles; they shall run and not be weary; they shall walk and not faint.

I know in my heart that someday Mr. Right will show, but until then I will continue to do Kingdom work and prepare myself for my King! I want God's best and when our hearts are turned towards God and not man, God will honor us for our faithfulness. I have consulted God many times in my life and I cannot recall him ever letting me down or not showing up on time. God is a good God and when He answers your prayer, He will do it in perfection!!!

Many of us make the mistake of going ahead of God. We make our own plans and then try to fit God in them and wonder later why things did not work out on our behalf. Many of us as women do not trust God when it comes to relationships. We feel that God must move around our biological clocks because if he does not then it will be too late. We tend to take and lean on the advice of society instead of dwelling on the word of God for sincere guidance and instruction. (Proverbs 3:

5&6) Trust in the Lord with all your heart and lean not unto your own understanding; In all your ways acknowledge him and he will direct your path. God has his best for us and is waiting to give it to us at the right time.

Jeremiah 29:11 says for I know the plans I have for you. Plans to prosper You and give you hope. Plans to give you a future of prosperity.

Matthew 6:33 – But seek ye first the Kingdom of God and his righteousness and all these things shall be added unto you.

Words of wisdom from my Godmother Prophet Lena Staton

God will never use a man his Spirit can never restrain. Why would we entertain dating someone, who does not surrender their life to your God? If they are rebellious how will you escape their lustful, luring, and cunning ways to trap you and cause you to compromise and lead you far from your commitment to Christ. Love God with all your heart, mind, and soul. No more slackness, or procrastination it is all or nothing. God is looking for those who absolutely love him. Hate what he hates and love what he loves. Praying in your prayer language will keep you abreast of what God is saying.

We must remember that the timing of God is especially important. He knows what we need and when we need it. We may feel we are ready to tie the knot, but there are things God knows about us, that even we ourselves do not know. He knows that if those areas of your life are not handled, then you will drag these issues into your marriage later. Waiting on God is important because the bible teaches us according to Psalm 33: 20

"That those who believe in **God** and have accepted His lordship over their lives **should wait** for Him. To **wait** for the **Lord** means to depend upon Him, to trust Him, to look unto Him. "**We** depend on the **LORD** alone to save us. Only he can help us, protecting us like a shield."

God does not move on our timing because He knows we do not know what is best for us. We choose our men from the physical (what he has, what he looks like, what he owns), but God looks at the heart of the man.

I am not saying we should settle for less. Please, please do not settle for less but settle for God's best. Pray for the kind of King you want in your life. Be specific, but do not be carnal with it. In other words, do not get in your flesh because your marriage will not be about you. It will be about him too! God knows each of us and He knows who to compare us with. Do not be so quick to choose the first fine, and handsome man, you lay your eyes on, because he could be a devil in disguise!!!

Be encouraged ladies and remember you are beautiful, a royal priesthood, a chosen generation, a peculiar people, you are daughters of the most, high God. You are expensive, worth more than a BMW, cost more than rubies and diamonds and hand crafted by God our awesome creator. Wait on God my friend. You are not alone. Remember, sometimes our desires may be delayed by God, but it does not mean he has denied us.

THE OUTCOME OF OUR CHOICES

After reading this book, please answer the following questions:

1. What should you do when making decisions in your life? A. Meditate and then decide? B. Ask the opinion of a friend first? C. Pray and seek God for the best answer for you.

   Why did you choose this answer?

   _____

   _____

2. Who are you?

   _____

   _____

3. What are you purposed to do? What are your special traits, qualities, strengths that God has placed inside of you to make an impact within the world in which we live?

   _____

   _____

4. Can you honestly say you are ready to be restrained by God? Yes _ or No _

   If you answered yes, explain in your own words what it means to be restrained by God?

   _____

   _____

5. Should sex come before or after marriage? Explain your answer:

_____

_____

6. How important are you to you? Do you value your worth? Yes_
    or No_

7. Fill in the blank.

    When a female respects her body and reverence her own stan-
    dards, it helps the male to

_____

_____

8. How does a female and male develop a soul tie? A. Having Sex
    B. Spending time together C. Becoming best friends

9. Based on your reading of this book, what is the danger in two
    unmarried people having a soul tie?

_____

_____

10. Based on your reading, what does God say about people having sex that are not married?

_____

_____

11. Based on the reading of this book, what can we as women do while waiting on Mr. Right?

_____

_____

_____

12. Why is it important for us as females to draw the line in our relationships with males?

_____

_____

_____

13. What is the danger in feeling lonely as a single woman?

_____

_____

14. What can we do when we feel our minds are being attacked by lustful thoughts or dreams?

_____

_____

15. On a scale from one to five with five being the highest and one being the lowest, how important is it that God connects you to the person he wants you to marry? Please circle the number of your choice. 1 2 3 4 5

Why did you choose this number?

_____

_____

16. On page 10, I wrote a statement by Priscilla Shirer. In your own words how did this statement affect you after reading it?

_____

_____

17. Now that you have completed reading this book, do you think you will approach your relationships differently or the same? Explain your answer

_____

_____

18. If you had a daughter and she was age eighteen and wanted to have sex, what would be your advice to her?

_____

_____

19. If you could erase your past of bad relationships with the opposite sex, do you think your attitude about sex before marriage would be the same or different? Why?

_____

_____

20. If you are waiting and looking forward to marriage, make a list of things you want from God in a marriage. Be specific and tell him what you want to see in your mate. Pray and get others you trust to believe in God with you for your desires.

_____

_____

CPSIA information can be obtained
at www.ICGtesting.com
Printed in the USA
LVHW011301191220
674520LV00005B/889